Liturgy and Allegory in Chretien's *Perceval*

by
Sister M. Amelia Klenke, O. P.

Copyright, 1951
University of North Carolina

Liturgy and Allegory in
Chretien's *Perceval*

IN a recent book-review, H. F. Williams wrote: "Just as for over a hundred years scholars had clung tenaciously, as a matter of faith almost, to the romantic theory of Germanic origins for the French epics —a theory founded on nothing more substantial than hypothesis and presumption, resting on myths now exploded, and supported by much faulty reasoning and analogy—so, for an equal length of time, modern critics have led long and happy lives finding one after another analogues of Arthurian material in Celtic stories. I would not deny them the pleasure they must find therein, but in view of the paucity of proof forthcoming, one wonders whether other lines of inquiry might not be more profitably conducted" (*Romance Philology*, II, [1949], 256). It is in complete accord with this view that the present investigation has been undertaken.

In his *Arthurian Tradition in Lambert d'Ardres*[1], Professor Holmes has again offered a brilliant lead. From Lambert's chronicle he notes that Arnoul the Elder went on the First Crusade and brought back to Ardres from Jerusalem some priceless relics, including a portion of the Lord's beard, a particle of the True Cross, and a piece of the rock from which the Saviour had ascended into Heaven. From Antioch Arnoul had retrieved what is described as *de lancea Domini;* the father of Arnoul the Elder had already donated to the Ardres church a small reliquary in which was, among other things, *de manna Domini*. The use of *de* (cf. also *de barba Domini* in the Lambert chronicle) suggests that the church possessed a portion of the lance, rather than the whole.

According to the *Catholic Encyclopedia*, St. Antoninus claimed in 570 to have seen the lance together with the Crown of Thorns in the basilica of Mt. Sion. In the Laurentian library at Florence, the Syriac manuscript dated 586 contains an illumination by Rabulas which shows Longinus piercing the side of Christ with his lance. Cassiodorus and Gregory of Tours testify that a spear was venerated in Jerusalem at the end of the sixth century. After Jerusalem was captured by the Persians in 614, the relic fell into pagan hands. A point of the lance was broken off and given to Nicetas who placed it in the church of St. Sophia in Constantinople. Several centuries later (1241), Baldwin II gave it to Louis IX together with the Crown of Thorns, and these relics were then deposited in the Sainte Chapelle of Paris. In the following century John Mandeville wrote that he had seen the blade both in Paris and in Constantinople, and that the latter relic was the larger of the two. This larger relic fell later into the hands of the Turks; and to insure the safety of his brother (a prisoner of the Pope), the sultan Bayezid II sent it to Innocent VIII. It is still preserved under the dome of St. Peter's.

The *Catholic Encyclopedia* goes on to say that at Rome there had been doubt about the authenticity of Bayezid's relic because of several counterclaims, including the supposed discovery of the *Holy Lance at Antioch, in 1098, during the First Crusade*: "It seems probable that it is identical with the relic now jealously preserved at Etschmiadzin in Armenia. This was never in any proper sense a lance, but rather the head of a standard, and (before its discovery under very questionable circumstances by the crusader Peter Bartholomew) it may conceivably have been venerated as the weapon with which certain Jews at Beirut struck a figure of Christ on the Cross; an outrage which was believed to have been followed by a miraculous discharge of blood." This association of the bleeding lance of Antioch with the Jews and with Beirut is doubly interesting because of the epithets used by Chrétien de Troyes concerning the Jews who took part in the Crucifixion[2] and because of his reference to this city when he describes the Grail Castle[3]. It is the more significant that a certain Foulque, of Arnoul's family, became lord of Beirut (cf. *Ardres* 102). It is perfectly understandable that the lance which later came to Ardres should have been taken, or thought to have been taken, from Jerusalem to Antioch for safekeeping. Christian teaching had been carried to Antioch by disciples from Cyprus and Cyrene who fled from Jerusalem during the persecution following the martyrdom of St. Stephen. It was only natural that the early Christians should have transported to Antioch as many of the sacred relics connected with the Passion as they could save, particularly after the fall of Jerusalem in 70 A.D.

In all likelihood Arnoul the Elder built at Ardres his fantastic castle with its "Solomon Chapel" as a sort of reliquary for the sacred treasures he had brought back from the crusade (cf. *Ardres* 102). Some fifty years later, Baldwin II was to follow his example at Guines when, presumably in 1169, he built his own "Solomon Chapel." Had Chrétien de Troyes ever seen the castle of Ardres? Situated barely twelve miles from the sea-coast and in close proximity to the Ardres canal, it would have served admirably as a model for the Grail Castle which Perceval finally found. But, even if Chrétien never saw the castle at Ardres, it is unlikely that he had not heard of its relics. He may well have been thinking of it when describing the Grail Castle, just as Rabelais was thinking of Chambord when writing about the Abbaye de Thélème. Lambert's chronicle is of primary importance to anyone interested in Chrétien's sources, as it leads directly or indirectly to the backdrop of Solomon's Temple in the *Perceval* poem. The chronicle yields valuable clues about the *manna* and the *bleeding lance*, two of the principal elements in the mystic Grail procession, and thereby gives support to a Judaeo-Christian interpretation of Chrétien's poem (cf. *Graal*, and also *infra*).

In the first half of the twelfth century, Bernard of Clairvaux had devoted a long series of sermons to the *Canticle of Canticles*. It is also of interest, and perhaps of significance for Chrétien, that Baldwin II, who became count of Ardres in 1169, was responsible for having the *Canticle* translated into French. The *Conte del Graal* was written about 1180. It will be remembered that Perceval sets out in the *springtime;* that *the trees are in blossom, the woods are in bud, the meadows are turning green,* and *the birds are warbling;* that the youth rejoices at the fine weather and the song of the birds. When he learns from a passing knight that a hauberk is a protection against javelins and arrows, Perceval retorts: "Sir knight, may God protect the *hinds* and the *stags* from such hauberks, for (unless He does) I could not kill any of them and would (therefore) never run after them" (*Perceval* 273-276). These elements in the poem invite comparison with the *Canticle of Canticles* (ii, 9-17): "My beloved is like a *roe*, or a young *hart*. . . . . Behold, my beloved speaketh to me: Arise, make haste, my love, my dove, my beautiful one, and come. For *winter is now past, the rain is over and gone. The flowers have appeared in our land,* the time of pruning is come: *the voice of the turtle* is heard in our land: the fig-tree hath put forth her *green* figs: the *vines in flower* yield their sweet smell . . . . Return: be like, my beloved, to a *roe*, or to a young *hart* upon the mountains of Bether." Of course, Chrétien's references to spring, birds, and flowers are part of a very familiar mediaeval literary baggage, but this does not preclude a conscious reminiscence of the *Canticle of Canticles*. It is well known, after all, that courtly poets, meridional and northern alike, were often thoroughly versed in Marial writings and traditions; consequently, it is not laboring a point to suggest that Chrétien's precise mention of hind and stag may imply more influence from the *Canticle* than from contemporary tradition in lyric poetry.

One of the most attractive passages in the *Perceval* poem is devoted to the tent of the sleeping damsel (vv. 637-655): "He (Perceval) was intent upon his riding until he saw a tent pitched in a beautiful meadow at the edge of a little brook. The tent was wondrously beautiful; one side was vermilion and the other was green, and trimmed with gold braid. On top there was a gilded eagle; the sun shone hard and bright upon the eagle, which was resplendent with dazzling vermilion. And all the meadows were illumined by the shining light from the tent. All around the tent, which was the fairest in the world, there were two arbors fashioned from boughs, and there were bowers designed as in Wales. The youth went toward the tent and said as he approached: 'Lord, now I behold Thy house.' "

The twentieth-century reader is frequently superficial in his attitude toward such passages. But, if willing to consider the possibility of a Judaeo-Christian interpretation of the poem, he may well ask himself: "Why the eagle? and has it any particular significance?" Together with the accent of mediaeval piety on the liturgy[4], three biblical passages acquire pertinence at this point:

> And they kept eight days with joy, after the manner of the feast of the tabernacles, remembering that not long before they had kept the feast of the tabernacles when they were in the mountains, and in dens, like wild beasts. Therefore, *they now carried boughs, and green branches* . . . . (*II Machabees* x, 6-7).
>
> *How beautiful are thy tabernacles, O Jacob, and thy tents, O Israel! As woody valleys, as watered gardens near the rivers, as tabernacles which the Lord hath pitched, as cedars by the water-side* (*Numbers* xxiv, 5-6).
>
> Let there be a trumpet in thy throat like *an eagle upon the house of the Lord* (*Osee* viii, 1).

It is scarcely coincidence that, when Perceval beholds the tent surmounted by the eagle, he exclaims: "Lord, now I behold Thy house."

Who is the beautiful damsel asleep in the tent, and from whom Perceval steals an emerald ring and some kisses? Perhaps the emerald affords another clue:

> And Judith seeing Holofernes sitting under a canopy, which was woven of purple and gold, with *emeralds* and other precious stones .... (*Judith* x, 19).

Emeralds are mentioned again and again in all manner of texts, yet it is not irrelevant to recall that Judith, who by her beauty and courage saved the Jewish race, is the prototype of the Virgin Mary, co-redemptrix of mankind. Some readers will doubtless be startled if it is suggested that the sleeping lady may indeed be Mary. In the *Apocalypse* there is the long-famous verse, which, incidentally, was the direct inspiration for Murillo's *Immaculate Conception*:

> And a great sign appeared in heaven: *A woman clothed with the sun*, and the moon under her feet, and on her head a crown of twelve stars (*Apocalypse* xii, 1).

This verse is followed by another not so well known:

> And there were given to the woman *two wings of a great eagle* that she might fly into the desert .... (*Apocalypse* xii, 14).

Surely this woman, sometimes referred to as Our Lady of Light, resembles the fair maid asleep in her tent which was surmounted by the eagle glittering in the sun[5].

In relating the life of the Cistercian mystic St. Lutgarde (1182-1246), her contemporary and biographer, Thomas de Cantimpré, describes her vision of St. John the Evangelist. In the vision, presumably at the beginning of her religious life, she beheld St. John as the "Eagle of Patmos, flying with plumage that so blazed with light that the whole world could have been illuminated by the glory of his wings" (*Wounds* 19). If Chrétien's eagle is by any chance a symbol of St. John, it gives one more reason to suppose that the sleeping lady may have been Mary; for the dying Christ had entrusted John and Mary to each other.

But there are further reasons for imagining that Chrétien may have had Mary in mind. Verses 672-676 say that the damsel was alone because her handmaids, according to their custom, had gone for fresh blossoms with which to strew the floor of the tent. Have not Mary's devotees down through the centuries gathered flowers to lay at her feet[6], and to weave into garlands with which to crown her? That she is linked with everything fairest in Nature is known to all, yet it is not superfluous to quote some charming lines from the different hours of the *Little Office of the Blessed Virgin Mary*:

> Like a vine, I gave forth a pleasant odor: and my flowers are the fruit of honor and riches (*Lauds*) .... I was exalted like the cedar in Libanus, and like a cypress-tree on Mount Sion: like a palm-tree in Cades was I exalted, and like a rose-plant in Jericho (*None*) .... O Virgin Mary, there is no one in the world born of

woman like to thee: flourishing like the rose, fragrant as the lily (*Compline*).

If in Chrétien's day Mary was ever designated as *Refuge of Sinners*, it would be the more significant that Perceval the sinner should have tarried with her awhile, and that he should have made his way to Christ through Mary's mediation. As Thomas Merton says (*Siloe* 29): "St. Bernard and his school were the greatest of the mediaeval panegyrists of the Mother of God.... They were the most explicit in proclaiming Mary as the mediatrix of all graces, through whom came all God's gifts to man." Also in this connection, it is pertinent to recall St. Bernard's famous sermon "De Aquaeductu," in *Nativitate B. V. Mariae* (cf. *Wounds* 25, note 17). It is all the more pertinent if perchance Chrétien ever did become a Cistercian. In any case, if the suggested identification with Mary is justified, then Chrétien is felicitous in the poetic reverence which leads him to have her bestow upon Perceval the mystic sword which it is tempting to consider as the gift, or the strengthening, of faith (cf. *infra*).

It is quite true that Chrétien has treated this whole episode with a certain désinvolture. In fact, it lends notable support to the hypothesis, so ably presented two decades ago by Mme Myrrha Lot-Borodine (cf. in particular, *Romania*, LVII, 198), that Chrétien was capable of attaining to no more than a "certaine spiritualité à mi-côte; rien de moins, rien de plus." She would undoubtedly say that the present monograph, like those of Eugène Anitchkof twenty and twenty-five years ago, "grandit de cent coudées le maître champenois." With full awareness of the risks and perils which attend any hypothesis about the mediaeval Grail, it is my firm conviction that Chrétien, even in the unfinished *Perceval* and without benefit of discredited Anitchkof theories, achieved a very special stature in his last years. In scholarship's common quest for the truth, the ultimate success of any one study must obviously depend on the subsequent findings and verdicts of qualified investigators. For the present, some of the conclusions here can be offered only very tentatively, while others are urged with a sense of virtual certainty: in any case, the reader remains a free and independent judge.

Again with reference to the episode of Perceval and the sleeping maiden, it may be suggested that, had not death overtaken Chrétien in the midst of his task, his conclusion to the poem might have partially explained his procedure. Also, it is evident from Perceval's words and actions that he is totally unaware of the maiden's identity. Because of his pride, his disobedience, and his lack of self-knowledge, he is still blinded to all spiritual values. His lack of reverence with the maid calls forth her stern rebuke, which may recall that Mary is also the *Mother of Fear*: "I am the Mother of fair love, and of fear and of knowledge and of holy hope" (*Compline: Little Office of the Blessed Virgin Mary*).

At this point, it is pertinent to return to the emerald which, by its color, is symbolic of hope. In the *Salve Regina*, written eighty or ninety years *before* Chrétien's time (cf. *Liturgia* 592), Mary is addressed as "vita, dulcedo, et spes nostra" (our life, our sweetness, and our hope). Because of Perceval's love for Mary (symbolized by the kiss)[7], and because of his hope (symbolized by the emerald), he will receive the grace of repentance. Let it be noted also that many virtues, including preservation of the wearer's chastity, were formerly ascribed to the emerald. It may be pointed out that later in the poem, despite latter-day interpretations of vv. 2054-2069, Perceval maintains his chastity while with Blancheflor: if he had not, surely any such transgression would not have been omitted from his subsequent sacramental confession to the hermit. This interpretation of the Blancheflor episode is discussed at more length in a note which is to appear in *Romance Philology*.

Because of its color, furthermore, the emerald was reputed to have the power of restoring sight; and it is the emerald which later helps to cure Perceval of the blindness which sin had brought to his soul; and, again, had he asked the vital question concerning the bleeding lance, the emerald might well have helped him to effect the cure of the lame Fisher King. It is well to remember here that Mary is the *Janua coeli* and that in the *Ave Maris Stella* she is the *felix coeli porta*, and that *Tobias* xiii, 21 records that "the gates of Jerusalem shall be built of sapphire, and of emerald."

There is a further passage, always applied to Mary, and present in Sext, None, and Lauds in the *Little Office of the Blessed Virgin Mary,*— a passage which argues still more for the Virgin as the sleeping maid in the tent, which (let it be repeated) the eagle symbolism and Perceval's very words have proclaimed to be the tent of the Lord: "God hath chosen her, and preferred her: and He maketh her to dwell in His tabernacle" (note that the words *tent* and *tabernacle* were often interchanged).

* * * *

Particularly helpful for this study is Professor Holmes's important "New Interpretation of Chrétien *Conte del Graal*" (cf. *supra*, note 1). His theory concerning the poem divides itself into three major parts: (1) Chrétien de Troyes was a converted Jew, also known as *Crestiens li Gois;* (2) his poem is an allegory in which the "Quest of the Holy Grail is the conversion of the Jewish Temple to Christianity;" (3) the lame Fisher King is Jacob, who was lame as a result of his struggle with the Angel of the Lord: he is also High Priest in the Grail Castle, a symbolical representation of the Temple of Solomon in Jerusalem[8].

Mr. Holmes is careful to indicate that Chrétien's possible conversion is proposed only as a suggestion, and by no means as demonstrated fact. Whatever Chrétien's origins and identity in real life, I believe it is quite possible that he might have partially identified himself with Perceval, in his search for ultimate truth. Furthermore, after studying the Dominican Holy Week services where the prayers for the conversion of the Jewish race play such an important rôle, I am firmly convinced that Mr. Holmes is far from having, as he puts it, "skidded with (the) whole structure."

If Chrétien's theme (cf. *infra*) was really the conversion of the Jewish race, and the Old Law giving way to the New, there is no place where he could have turned more profitably for inspiration than to the liturgy[9] for Holy Week, particularly for Holy Thursday and Good Friday. Here, too,

Chrétien would find his ideal setting for the procession of the Holy Grail; here he surely found a host of his symbols, each with its connotation according to the Old and New Laws (cf. *infra*).

Two objections will arise immediately against comparison of the *Perceval* with Dominican liturgy: (1) it is unlikely that the particular liturgical usage which Chrétien was following will ever be identified; (2) the poem was written before 1181, whereas the Dominicans were not canonically established until 1215. While variations abound among the different usages, the *essentials* in the observances and offices for Holy Week are common to all. The very fact of the many points of contact between the poem and the Dominican liturgy is in itself an adequate guarantee, and without benefit of circular reasoning. In other words, it is far less important to determine the specific liturgy which Chrétien utilized than it is to clarify and underscore the richness of liturgical background in his poem. It is with the second and larger of these objectives that this study is concerned.

As for the validity of following here a liturgy which, in a formal sense, postdates the *Perceval*, it need only be remembered that the first Dominicans made use of the Roman Rite as they found it observed in the Diocese of Toulouse, and that, "as regards the paschal season, the Dominican office was remarkable, for it adopted and for many centuries retained some very ancient Roman customs." This is made abundantly clear by Father William Bonniwell, O.P., in his *History of the Dominican Liturgy* (New York, 1944; cf., in particular, pp. 21, 144). In *The Office of Holy Week according to the Dominican Rite* (edition of 1904; p. 82), also known as *The Dominican Holy-Week Book*, it is pointed out that "the Tenebrae Offices for Maundy Thursday, Good Friday, and Holy Saturday, which in the primitive ages were said at a very early hour in the mornings of those days, are now said or sung (by way of anticipation) on Wednesday, Thursday and Friday evening. At the close of each psalm, both at Matins and Lauds, *Gloria Patri* is omitted, and one of the fifteen candles in the triangular candlestick is extinguished."

Further pertinent information is provided by Dom Gaspar Lefebvre, O.S.B., in his edition of the *Saint Andrew Daily Missal* (Saint Paul, Minnesota, 1943; p. 208):

> The celebrations and ceremonies of . . . . Holy Week have their origin in the Church at Jerusalem. There, with the Holy Gospels in hand, the Christians would follow their Redeemer, step by step, piously gathering on the very spot precious souvenirs of the most solemn among all events, that which marked the close of His mortal life.
>
> These celebrations, at first local in character, were adopted into the liturgy at Rome, where the very churches were planned in such a manner as to make it possible to carry out the offices of Holy Week in the way that had been customary in Jerusalem. The last three days are called the Sacred Triduum.

When it is observed that the crucifix itself is veiled, we see here a trace of the custom which obtained of suspending a curtain between the sanctuary and the nave, during the whole of Lent. (*This Lenten curtain or cortina is still used in the Cistercian liturgy and others.*) In those times, public penitents who had been excluded from the Church could not enter it again until Holy Thursday, and when this custom was abolished, all Christians were more or less placed in the position of such penitents. Although no sentence of exclusion was pronounced against them, the sanctuary and all that took place there was hidden from them, to show that they could only merit the share in Eucharistic worship given them in their Easter Communion, after they had brought forth fruits worthy of penance. (*Note how effectively this fits in with the Holmes theory that Perceval, or "Perce-voile," was unable to pierce the veil of the mystery because of his sinful state.*) [10]

Finally, by stripping the altars and silencing all organs and bells from the Gloria of Holy Thursday until the Gloria of Holy Saturday, the Church gives expression to the grief which she feels at the memory of the death of her divine spouse. (*This recalls the silence maintained during the mystic Grail procession, but only as possible reminiscence, and certainly not as demonstration.*)

In order to go beneath the surface of Chrétien's story, it is useful to attempt an analysis of its symbolism, even at the risk of error in points of detail. My ideas, if accepted, can well be synthesized with those of Mr. Holmes; and, in any case, the conclusions arrived at here must rest upon the solid foundation he has laid.

He has formulated his belief (*Graal* 14-15) that St. Paul's Epistle to the Hebrews was the inspiration for Chrétien's version of the quest of the Holy Grail. As he points out, this Epistle "is basically a comparison between Judaism and Christianity stating that Judaism is 'only the earthly shadow of the heavenly realities that Jesus Christ came to establish and bring within our reach.' The priesthood of Christ is contrasted with the Levitical priesthood." Perhaps the best illustration of this idea, and the most significant in giving a key to the meaning of the *Perceval*, is taken from the Maundy Thursday Matins:

As we are beginning, dearly beloved, the commemoration of the Lord's passion, we can see why it was provided in the divine counsels that the sacrilegious princes of the Jews, and the wicked priests, who had often sought opportunity to rage against Christ, should only upon the Paschal feast have the power of venting their fury to the full. For it was fitting that the mysteries which had long been foreshadowed should be fulfilled in a public manner; and that the various victims with their different meanings should be summed up and expressed in one great sacrifice. In order, therefore, that the shadows might yield to the substance, and the symbols to the reality, the Old Law was consummated in a new sacrament, the victim is changed into the Host, and Blood abolishes the sacrifices of blood: and thus, whilst being changed, the legal festival is fulfilled. (*Seventh Sermon of Pope Leo IX on the Passion*)

Concerning the Holy Week services, a number of passages from Dom Lefebvre's commentary in the *Saint Andrew Daily Missal* (pp. 206, 270-271, 285) are of interest:

It was at the end of Lent, when the Church makes remembrance of the death and triumph of Christ, that the ancient councils required that the sacraments of Baptism, Confirmation and the Eucharist should be given to the catechumens and that public penitents should be reconciled by sacramental absolution. (*It will be remembered that Perceval makes his sacramental confession to the hermit on Good Friday.*) In a sense these catechumens were 'buried' together with Christ by baptism into death and rose with Him to newness of life. So do Passiontide and Easter, by marking for all Christians the anniversary of the reception of those blessings, remind them that Our Lord's Passion and Resurrection were at once the efficient cause and the pattern of their own, and help them as the years pass, to share in these sacred mysteries in an ever more full and intimate way. These feasts were not, a mere commemoration, concerned only with our Lord Himself; they become a reality for His whole mystical body.

The Liturgy of Maundy Thursday formerly provided for the celebration of three Masses: 1) for the reconciliation of public penitents, 2) for the consecration of the holy oils, 3) for a special commemoration of the institution of the Holy Eucharist at the last supper. This last Mass is the only one that has been preserved and at it the bishop, attended by twelve priests, seven deacons and seven subdeacons, blesses the holy oils in his Cathedral church.

The Church, endowed with the power of laying down the conditions necessary for the validity of the Sacrament of Penance, required in the first centuries, that after open confession of sins of public notoriety, described by the Fathers of the Church as capital sins, the absolution should be preceded by the complete fulfilling of the satisfaction or penance. Hence the rite of the reconciliation of penitents, who on Maundy Thursday received the sacramental absolution of the sins for which they had done public penance during Lent. To this may be traced the Easter Confession following the forty days' penance....

The blessing of the holy oils took place with a view to the baptism and confirmation of the catechumens during Easter night. (*This suggests that, had Chrétien finished his poem with the conversion of Jacob, he would presumably have concluded with the joyous and trimphant liturgy for Easter Sunday. Cf. infra, note 16.*)

On Maundy Thursday the Church lays special stress on the institution of the Holy Eucharist and of the priesthood. (*How natural a source for Chrétien to select as background for the Grail procession and for the conversion of the high priest Jacob.*) After the Mass, the altar is stripped in order to show that the Holy Sacrifice is interrupted and will not be offered up again to God until Holy Saturday. The priest therefore consecrates two hosts, for on Good Friday the Church refrains from renewing on the altar the sacrifice of Calvary.

On Good Friday the priest wears black vestments—often trimmed with purple. (*It will be remembered that Jacob is also dressed in black with purple edging.*) The Station is held at the basilica in Rome which represents Jerusalem. It is consecrated to the Passion of our Lord, and contains earth from Calvary, important fragments of the True Cross, and one of the nails. On this day, the anniversary of our Saviour's death, the Church gives her temples an appearance of desolation and clothes her ministers in mourning (*and 'mourning' is the precise word used in Graal 17 to describe and account for Jacob's sable garments*). The first part of the liturgy for Good Friday, the Mass of the Catechumens, consists, like the first part of any Mass, in prayers, readings and chants: it recalls the gatherings held by the Jews in the synagogue, and also by the early Christians.

None being ended in choir, the priest and his ministers, in black vestments, without lights or incense, go up to the altar where they prostrate themselves and pray for a few moments. Then begins the Mass of the Catechumens.

This Mass of the Catechumens is followed by the Solemn Prayers for the needs of the Church, which are edited as follows by Dom Lefebvre:

Let us pray also for our catechumens: that our Lord God would open the ears of their hearts, and the gate of his mercy: that having received by the laver of regeneration, the remission of all their sins *(which makes one think of Perceval)*, they may also belong to our Lord Jesus Christ.

Almighty and everlasting God, who always makest thy Church fruitful in new children: increase the faith and understanding of our catechumens: that being regenerated in the waters of baptism, they may be admitted into the society of thy adopted children.

Let us pray, beloved brethren, to God the Father Almighty, that he would purge the world of all errors: cure diseases: drive away famine: open prisons: break chains: grant a safe return to travellers *(which is a reminder of the pilgrim Perceval, and of his experiences with the camp of Blancheflor)*: and a secure haven to such as are at sea.

Let us pray also for heretics and schismatics *(Clamadeus and Anguingueron? Cf. infra)*, that our Lord God would be pleased to to deliver them from all errors: and recall them to our holy Mother the Catholic and Apostolic Church *(Perceval's mother? Cf. infra)*.

Almighty and everlasting God, who savest all, and wilt have no one perish: look on the souls that are seduced by the deceit of the devil *(Anguingueron?)*: that the hearts of those that err, having put away all heretical malice, may repent and return to the unity of thy truth *(Blancheflor? Cf. infra).*

Let us pray also for the perfidious Jews *(cf. supra, note 2)* that our Lord would withdraw the veil *(Perce-voile? cf. supra, note 10)* from their hearts that they may acknowledge our Lord Jesus Christ *(which Perceval does from v. 6509 on).*

Almighty and everlasting God, Who deniest not thy mercy even to the perfidious Jews: hear our prayers which we pour forth for the blindness of that people: that by acknowledging the light of thy truth, which is Christ, they may be brought out of their darkness. Through the same Lord *(cf. Perceval's confession: "Sire, for five years I have not known where I have been; I neither loved God nor believed in God, nor in that time have I ever done aught but evil." Perceval, vv. 6364-6367).*

These prayers for the Jews obviously recall the Matins for Good Friday, and "All the ends of the earth shall remember, and shall be converted to the Lord" *(Psalm* xxi, 28), not to mention the Lessons taken from the Lamentations of the prophet Jeremias, for which the reader is advised to consult verses 1-9 of chapter ii. Verse 6 in this biblical chapter, concerning king and priest, is suggestive of Jacob as high priest and Fisher King (cf. *Graal* 13). Verse 7, in the same chapter, might be an explanation of the spell on the Grail Castle (cf. *Graal* 13). Citations from Bible and liturgy could be multiplied, more or less indefinitely, in support of the hypotheses which Mr. Holmes has already advanced so persuasively, but it would be idle to reproduce these in detail, inasmuch as his particular suggestions about Chrétien's poem do not stand in need of reënforcement from other students of the Grail tradition.

It is desirable, however, to remind ourselves again of Mr. Holmes's conclusions that the Grail, the lance, the blood, the silver plate, and the feminine figures in the Grail procession were the vessel of manna, Aaron's rod, the sacrificial blood made by the high priest, the tablet of the law, and the maidens whom Chrétien associated with the two cherubim in the Holy of Holies (cf. *Graal* 13-14). It is perfectly conceivable that the lame Fisher King (= Jacob?) and Perceval should have regarded these symbols in this light before the former's conversion from Judaism, and before the latter's conversion from sin. Mr. Holmes has implied[11] that with the dissolution of the Grail Castle these Jewish symbols would be transformed into the chalice, the lance of Longinus, the blood of Christ, the paten used at Mass over the chalice, and adoring angels *(Graal* 28) ministering to the Sacrament which has been prefigured by the manna. After all, there are repeated references to these symbols in the liturgy for Holy Thursday and Good Friday.

In connection with the bleeding lance, is it not possible that its bearer in the Grail Procession is, in reality, Longinus, although unrecognized by Jacob (because of his lack of faith) or by Perceval (because of his spiritual blindness)? Is it not then conceivable that, had Perceval asked the requisite question about the lance, Longinus's account of his own conver-

sion would have effected that of Jacob and the Jewish Temple? That the
Jews would have been cured of their blindness just as Longinus had been
(literally as well as figuratively)?

It is quite possible that Perceval and Jacob regarded the lance under
the aspect of the Jewish Law. The Good Friday *Lauds* include the following from the Prophecy of *Habacuc* (iii, 11): "The sun and the moon stood
still in their habitation, in the light of thy arrows, they shall go in the
brightness of thy glittering spear." This spear may also be associated with
the Mass of the Catechumens of Good Friday where, in the Second Lesson,
the priest reads from *Exodus* (xii, 3-11): "Let every man take a lamb . . . .
And they shall take of the blood thereof, and put it upon the side posts, and
on the upper door posts of the houses, wherein they shall eat it . . . and thus
you shall eat it; You shall gird your reins, and you shall have shoes on your
feet, holding staves in your hands." In the Passion of St. John (xix, 33-
35), which is read during the Good Friday Mass: "But after they were
come to Jesus, when they saw that he was already dead, they did not
break his legs. But one of the soldiers with a spear opened his side, and
immediately there came out blood and water. And he that saw it, hath
given testimony; and his testimony is true. And he knoweth that he saith
true; that you also may believe." Thus, whether the lance is regarded
under the aspect of the Old Law or under that of the New, it is associated
with the spilling of the blood of the Paschal victim, and it must be viewed
in connection with the conversion of the Jews. Therefore, the symbol
chosen by Chrétien seems admirably fitted to his needs; and its importance
in the Grail Procession inclines all the more to the belief that the quest was
indeed the conversion of the Jewish Temple to Christianity.

After the Prayers for the Needs of the Church, there follows the ceremony of the Adoration of the Cross, in which Perceval actually partic-
ipated[12]. Here again are telling parallels to Chrétien's symbols:

> My people, what have I done to thee? or in what have I grieved
> thee? Answer me.
>
> Because I brought thee out of the land of Egypt: thou hast pre-
> pared a Cross for thy Saviour . . . .
>
> Because I led thee through the desert forty years: and fed thee
> with manna, and brought thee into an excellent land, thou hast pre-
> pared a Cross for thy Saviour . . . .
>
> What more could I do for thee, that I have not done? I planted
> thee a most beautiful vine: and thou hast proved exceeding bitter
> to me: for in my thirst thou gavest me vinegar to drink: and with
> a spear thou hast pierced the side of thy Saviour.

Is it mere coincidence that here in the liturgy are, in such close proximity,
references to the Crucifixion, the spear, and the manna? Chrétien has re-
verted to the Crucifixion twice in his tale, in places of special prominence:
once at the beginning of the poem when Perceval's mother exhorts him
to lead a good life (cf. vv. 580-591), and again when the pilgrims encounter
him dressed in his armor on Good Friday (cf. vv. 6266-6296).

During the Adoration of the Cross, the *Crux Fidelis* is sung, and here are more reminders of Longinus and the Fisher King:

4   And where the traitor gave the wound
    There healing remedies are found ....
8   Gall was his drink; his flesh they tear
    With thorns and nails; a cruel spear
    Pierces his side, from whence a flood
    Streams forth, of water mixed with blood.

After the Adoration, the procession is formed to bring back the Blessed Sacrament from the Repository where it has been placed after the Holy Thursday Mass. Candles are lighted, and when the priest has received from the deacon the chalice containing the Host (the *oiste* in the poem, and which had been prefigured by the manna), he stands up and turns towards the people. After the *Tantum Ergo*, the procession moves to the high Altar while the *Vexilla Regis* is sung: ". . . . A cruel spear let out a flood of water mixed with saving blood, Which gushing from the Saviour's side Drown'd our offenses in the tide . . . ."

It is, however, unnecessary to labor the theory of liturgical inspiration for the Grail procession, especially since Mme Lot-Borodine's comparative analysis of Chrétien's version with eastern and occidental liturgies (cf. *Romania*, LVII [1931], 169-196). Her conclusion is solidly established: "Le rite eucharistique poétisé, compliqué à souhait et teinté sans doute de souvenirs légendaires par le trouvère champenois, est, au demeurant, un rite de l'Eglise romaine." Except that Chrétien might conceivably have heard notions about Byzantine liturgy from returning crusaders, Mme Lot-Borodine shows that there can have been little or no thought in Chrétien's mind of either Byzantine or Gallican rite.

As for the Grail procession, it remains only to add a note about the candles (vv. 3213-3219) and the *tailleor d'arjant* (v. 3231). As Mr. Holmes has observed (*Graal* 17), the ten golden candlesticks of *II Paralipomenon* (iv, 7) "surely did not mean ten-branched candelabra in the Temple of Solomon, but a mediaeval reader might be pardoned for interpreting in that way," but, again, the only essential here is the liturgical accent in Chrétien's description[13]. The *tailleor* is taken to be a "sheet or plate of silver" (*Graal* 12), intended perhaps to receive the blood falling from the lance (Mme Lot-Borodine, *loc. cit.*, p. 190; but compare with vv. 3198-3201, 3230-3231, 3565-3567!). Although there would be nothing to *require* a paten among the *res sacrae* in the Grail procession, there is equally little reason for assuming that the *tailleor* of Chrétien's fancy did not resemble one. Moreover, Mme Lot-Borodine's citation (*loc. cit.*, p. 189, note 2) does not mean that a silver paten could not be used with a gold ciborium; different metals are admissible together to-day, just as in the twelfth century.

It seems inevitable that Chrétien drew from the Holy Week liturgy in his treatment of the Blessed Sacrament, and of the priesthood as symbolized by Jacob. In all Maundy Thursday ceremonies, the Church lays special stress on the Holy Eucharist and the priesthood. By underscoring the vital question which Perceval failed to ask regarding the Grail and the lance, Chrétien

has emphasized his evident concern with this liturgical season. Professor
A. H. Schutz has remarked (cf. *Graal* 21) that "in the Haggadah tradition the Passover ceremony begins with four questions that must be asked by the youngest person (=the greatest fool?)." Thus it may be inferred that the basic interest of the Grail question would stem from very ancient tradition.

The poem makes it clear (cf. vv. 3593-3595, 6392-6401) that Perceval, in his state of sin for abandoning his mother and thus causing her death, is unable to ask the Grail question. Although his mother gave him her blessing, with consent implied (vv. 617-619), as he was leaving, the sin which he was committing was none the less "mortal"; for he had gone only the distance of *le giet d'une pierre menue* (v. 621) when he saw that she had fallen in a death-like faint, yet he went on his way without a further word. The three elements necessary for mortal sin are clearly present: grievous matter, sufficient reflection, full consent of the will.

With real psychological insight, Chrétien has developed the character of Perceval with all its weaknesses: he is proud, self-sufficient, and disobedient. Very near the beginning of the poem, Perceval remembers that his mother had instructed him to cross himself in a certain situation, *"mes cest anseing desdeignerai"* (v. 119). Perceval is disrespectful, headstrong, and indifferent to things of the spirit: when his mother explains what she has suffered, "the youth understands very little of what his mother says to him. 'Give me something to eat,' he answers, 'I know nothing of what you (are trying to) tell me; but right gladly would I go to the king who makes knights, and I shall go, no matter who is distressed'" (vv. 489-495). It is only gradually that Chrétien has Perceval acquire awareness of his fault: glimmerings of remorse are reflected in his talk with Gornemant (cf. vv. 1580-1592), but at the end of the first quarter of Perceval's story it is only good psychology that his conscience is just beginning to awaken and to understand.

If the identity of Perceval's mother were known, the gravity of the sin might stand out more clearly. She is obviously Christian, for she has instructed her son concerning God, the angels, and the devil. She has taught him to pray whenever he comes to a church, and it is she who has taught him the prayers he recites when he mistakes the knights for angels. Given the orthodoxy of her admonitions to Perceval together with the fact that she lives in the *gaste forest* (the Waste Forest of the White Monks[14]), may she not possibly represent the spirit of contemplation, or vocation to the Religious Life? and may not her words which Perceval is forever quoting, to Gornemant's disgust, be symbolic of the commandments and precepts of the Church? and does Perceval's departure, therefore, represent his resistance to grace? does this explain the real grievousness of his sin? For the present, however, it must be admitted that it is not possible to feel anything like certainty about any identification of Perceval's mother.

At the time of the Grail procession and the banquet, Perceval makes no sacramental communion; nor could he have received the Blessed Sacrament "with a pure heart."[15] There is, however, an important parallel between the banquet and *Hebrews* ix (cf. *Graal* 14) :

> Into the first tabernacle the priests indeed always entered, accomplishing the offices of sacrifices. But into the second, the high priest alone, once a year: not without blood, which he offereth for his own, and the people's ignorance: the Holy Ghost signifying this, that the way into the holies was not yet made manifest, whilst the former tabernacle was yet standing. Which is a parable of the time present: according to which gifts and sacrifices are offered, which can not, as to the conscience, make him perfect that serveth, only in meats and in drinks, and divers washings, and justices of the flesh laid on them until the time of correction (vv. 6-10).

This passage is not taken into account by Mario Roques in his introduction to Lucien Foulet's translation of the *Perceval* (Paris, 1947; pp. xxiv-xxvi) where, despite Mme Lot-Borodine, Chrétien would seem to have "imaginé la combinaison de la procession grecque et de la nourriture spirituelle du reclus." However, while maintaining that there is some sort of communion at the Grail Castle, Roques naturally recognizes that it is something outside regular church practice. Perceval does not receive the actual Sacrament until, by his confession to the hermit, he has at last attained grace: note also that the familiar words from *I Corinthians* (xi, 28) are in the Epistle read at Mass on Holy Thursday—"But let a man prove himself: and so let him eat of that bread, and drink of the chalice[16]."

The Holy Week liturgy furnishes various passages which are suggestive of Perceval as the sinner; while no one of these by itself is impressive as a parallel, the following have collective significance as reminders of Chrétien's undoubted familiarity with the liturgy as a whole:

> Why, O unhappy Judas, not take advantage of such love? Lo, the Lord spares thy audacity, and to no one but to thyself does Christ make thee known; neither thy name nor thy person is discovered (*Perceval does not know his name until he makes the right guess, in v. 3575, after he has left the Grail Castle*), but by the word of truth and mercy thine inmost heart is struck. Neither the honour of the apostolate nor the communion of the sacraments is denied thee. Return to your senses and shake off this mad folly: repent, for mercy invites thee, salvation urges thee, and the Life recalls thee to life (*Maundy Thursday Matins, Lesson VI of the Second Nocturn*).

> Say, why dost thou (=*Judas*) betray him? Perhaps because he gave thee power over the devils, and taught thee to cure the sick (*cf. Perceval's failure to cure the Fisher King*).—(St. John Chrysostom, quoted in the *Third Nocturn of the Maundy Thursday Matins, Lesson VII*).

> Christ offered him (=*Judas*) the Blood which he had sold; that he might have forgiveness of his sins, if only he would repent. For

Christ merited for him the communication of the sacrifice (*Maundy Thursday Matins, Lesson VIII*).

.... Who have said to God: Depart from us, we desire not the knowledge of thy ways (*Job* xxi, 14; and included at end of Maundy Thursday *Matins*).

In connection with the last of the four passages just cited, it will be remembered that Perceval confesses (vv. 6364-6367) that for five years he has neither loved God nor believed in Him, that he had in fact forgotten God (v. 6383). On the other hand, it would be excessive to seek parallels between the Judas kiss and the kisses which Perceval steals from the sleeping damsel in the tent.

Perceval's quest for understanding and salvation brings to mind certain verses from the Psalms in the Holy Thursday and Good Friday Matins: "I studied that I might know this thing (*lance and Grail?*), it is a labour in my sight: until I go into the sanctuary of God, and understand concerning their last ends" (*Psalm* lxxii, 16-17).—"One thing I have asked of the Lord . . . . that I may see the delight of the Lord, and may visit his temple . . . . In the day of evils, he hath protected me in the secret place of his tabernacle (*cf. vv. 6481-6491 of the poem, where the hermit whispers a prayer to Perceval, who is to use it only in moments of great peril*) . . . . My father and mother have left me: but the Lord hath taken me up" (*Psalm* xxvi, 4-10).

Cruden's *Concordance* has several columns of references to *sword(s)* in the Bible, but even in the absence of clear-cut parallels, it would be tempting to suppose that Chrétien has used Perceval's sword as a symbol of Faith and, perhaps, of the Sacrament of Confirmation. Perceval has done nothing to merit the sword which comes to him as an unsought gift from the blond maiden (=*la sore pucele*, his niece; v. 3145). Faith also is a gift freely given. Perceval learns (vv. 3140-3141) that his new sword is proof against all perils save one, and (vv. 3154-3155) that there are only two other swords like it. The three swords were forged by the same smith, Trebuchet (v. 3679), a word which could mean "assaying scales," which might in turn symbolize God's Justice (cf. *Graal* 22 and *Deuteronomy* xxxii, 4).

The possibility that Perceval's sword might symbolize Confirmation is admittedly tenuous. Yet this Sacrament, and Baptism as well, used to be administered on Easter night, after the blessing of the Holy Oils on Maundy Thursday[17].

Saint Paul often alludes to Faith as a shield, a breastplate, the armor of light, the armor of God. It is reasonable to guess that, if Perceval's sword is Faith, then the other two fashioned by Trebuchet are Hope and Charity[18]. Also, Chrétien's special concern with charity in his prologue (vv. 43-59) readily recalls Saint Paul's "the greatest of these . . . ." On the other hand, whether or not Perceval's sword denotes Faith, it can fail him in only one situation: Trebuchet's other two swords are identical, so must it be assumed that Hope and Charity can each fail one in but a single situation? The question is entered for record, if only to remind the reader that no identification of Perceval's sword is considered here as more than an appealing suggestion. Also, a further question may be entered for record, but again without advocacy in any direction: could the principles of mediaeval rhetoric imply that the prologue enshrouds the author's *intentio*, that Perceval is fallen so low because of childish lack of love for his mother and for his God?

The possibilities and doubts about identification of Perceval's sword with Faith must be set beside Mr. Holmes's suggestion (*Graal* 21) that "if Christ is as a sword, there are two others like it, the Father and the Holy Ghost." In terms of divine omnipotence, is this a more satisfactory interpretation of the circumstance that the sword can fail Perceval in any situation, even though in only one such instance? The one situation is, of course, the fact of Perceval's state of mortal sin. Are not all three, Faith and Hope and Charity, more likely, in any circumstance, to fail than the Persons of the Trinity? Thus, Mr. Holmes has discussed elements of ultimately divine efficacy, but does it necessarily follow that these establish the identifications which Chrétien's mediaeval reader was expected to recognize? At the same time, if, in any of the poet's imaginings, the Persons of the Trinity might have chosen (or might have been thought) to "fail," then Mr. Holmes is manifestly nearer the answer, despite other present-day arguings for different solution(s): on the other hand, if Faith and Hope and Charity, all three, may each allow one and yet only one failure on the part of a single individual (*e.g.*, Perceval in his awkward formative stages, and, for that matter, during most of his story), then the sword may still stand for Faith. In any event, no positive claim is made, either in this study or in Mr. Holmes's, that the *non liquet* stage has yet been passed. In fact, Chrétien may have been thinking of something quite different from anything which any modern critic has thus far suspected. Finally, however, one may be certain that, whatever Chrétien's intent in his symbolism of the sword, there is nothing which could be remotely inconsistent with the Holy Week liturgy. It remains, therefore, to add but one brief note concerning Perceval's sword, a note which, by the way, reëmphasizes the excellence of Mr. Holmes's monograph (cf. *Graal* 22, 34): when Perceval hears from the maid with her headless knight that his sword will fail him on one occasion, he asks where it can (*au besoin*) be repaired; she tells him of the *"lac qui est sor Cotoatre"* (v. 3675; and note the rhyme with *rebatre*). Convincingly, Mr. Holmes takes the lake to be Galilee and Cotoatre to be *Kattath* (or rather, *Cateth*: cf. *Josue* xix, 15), one of the twelve cities in the inheritance of the tribe of the children of Zabulon. Cateth would obviously be a suitable place for the sword of wavering faith to be repaired and strengthened. But the *non liquet* is still, unfortunately, quite intact.

The theory has been advanced (*Graal* 21) that Perceval's scarlet cloak is symbolic of sin, but the fact that four *valets* appear and wrap Perceval in the *mantel d'escarlate* (vv. 3073-3074) at the Grail Castle raises a doubt. Might not the mantle be equally well considered as a cloak of love (red is also symbolic of love) which the four *valets*, in the service of the Fisher King (=Jacob?), were giving as a mark of their master's affection? Among Biblical references to scarlet are the following:

(Aaron and his sons) shall spread over (the table of proposition) a cloth of scarlet (*Numbers* iv, 8).

Ye daughters of Israel, weep over Saul, who clothed you with scarlet in delights (*II Kings* i, 24).

And stripping him (Christ), they (Pilate's soldiers) put a scarlet cloak about him (*Matthew* xxvii, 28).

For I saw among the spoils a scarlet garment exceeding good (*Josue* vii, 21).

And the woman was clothed round about with purple and scarlet, and gilt with gold (*Apocalypse* xvii, 4).

That great city, which was clothed with fine linen, and purple, and scarlet, and was gilt with gold (*Apocalypse* xviii, 16).

He. They that were fed delicately have died in the streets; they that were brought up in scarlet have embraced the dung (*Lamentations of Jeremias* iv, 5; included in the Holy Saturday *Matins*).

The implications of opulence and royalty are evident in these passages, but it is the last one (in the Holy Saturday Matins) which, taken in entirety, fits exactly with my present conception of Perceval.

If there is ever any certainty about the identity of Perceval's mother, it will be easier to discuss the significance of the coarse garments which she had given him, and which he was loath to put aside (cf., e.g., vv. 1147-1191). Perceval's "refusal to abandon his simple clothing is emphasized over and over, so that we can be certain it had some meaning for Chrétien" (*Graal* 23)[19]. Eventually (vv. 1597-1623), Gornemant de Goort, persuasively identified with Ecclesiastes (*Graal* 23-24), induces Perceval to give up his modest costume. If the latter's mother represented vocation to the Religious Life, this costume might signify either the Vow of Poverty or the Virtue of Humility. But, when Perceval yields to Gornemant's advice, he shows no signs of possessing these virtues, yet toward the end of the *Perceval* story humility is precisely the virtue which is extolled and recommended to him by the hermit (cf. v. 6464). The interplay of the several points reviewed in this paragraph shows again how firmly scholarship, for Chrétien's *Perceval*, is still anchored at the *non liquet* level. It is clear that, on the one hand, Perceval's mother acted with good intent in giving him only coarse garments, and that, on the other hand, the *prodon* Gornemant (whom Chrétien calls *li sages* in v. 1653) has the poet's approval for his influence on the "hero" of the narration. Whatever identifications are still to be determined, it is also clear that Perceval's costume in the first verses of the poem is appropriate at that stage in his moral formation, while Gornemant's view matches Perceval's arrival at the beginning of the "second quarter" in his long journey to ultimate grace. Merely by way of postscript query at this point: is it possible that Gornemant (*if* he is Ecclesiastes) represents a spirituality which, while involving no more goodness or piety than one recognizes in the unalloyed loyalty and devotion of Perceval's mother, forwards his quest in a manner over and beyond her resources?

A few trial-balloon hypotheses are now proposed in the closing pages of this monograph. No one is more aware than the author that these remaining suggestions are tenuous, but it is hoped that they may lay a foundation for more conclusive interpretations in the future. In any case, the following paragraphs should serve to reëmphasize the importance of Holy Week liturgy in the plan and details of the *Perceval*.

There may be hints in the liturgy concerning the identity of the *Orgueilleux de la Lande*, who rebukes (cf. vv. 3835-3898) Perceval and the damsel in the tent, from whom he had stolen the emerald and many kisses; the *Orgueilleux* accuses her unjustly of lack of chastity, and then oppresses her. For instance, what of the "oppressor" (*calomniateur* in the French translation offers another parallel, inasmuch as the knight accuses the lady wrongly) in *Psalm* lxxi, 4; and the pride which "hath held them fast" in *Psalm* lxxii, 6? Chrétien's vaguer rememberings? Probably so, but the two Psalms just cited figure in the Second Nocturn of Holy Thursday Matins.

Further study of Chrétien's use of proper names[20] must be carried through on an extensive scale if the true meaning of the poem is ever to be clarified in full. For example, does Blancheflor who weeps over Perceval during the night (cf. vv. 1964-1969) represent Jerusalem under the Old Law? Lesson I in the Holy Thursday Matins includes the following from the *Lamentations of Jeremias* (i, 2): "Weeping she (=Jerusalem) hath wept in the night, and her tears are on her cheeks: there is none to comfort her among all them that were dear to her." And what is the significance of the name *Belrepaire*[21] for her abode? Under the New Law could Blancheflor stand for the purity of Christian doctrine, for which so many had laid down their lives[22]? And could her enemies, Clamadeus and Ang(u)ing(u)-eron (Accuser of God, and Deceiver, respectively: cf. *Graal* 26), be merely symbols of the various heresies and schisms which Bishop Foulque and the first Dominicans were laboring (not long after the *Perceval* was written) to suppress?

Is there a possibility that Perceval's uncle (i.e., brother of his mother and of the hermit; cf. vv. 3242, 6413-6431) might be the prophet Elias, the prototype of Christ whom Zachary calls the future "prophet of the Highest" (*Luke* i, 76)? In the poem this personage, at the Grail Castle, occupies an inner chamber where he is served nothing but the *oiste*. Like Christ in the Sacrament, Elias is associated with the tabernacle: "And Peter answering, said to Jesus .... if thou wilt, let us make here three tabernacles, one for thee, one for Moses, and one for Elias" (*Matthew* xvii, 4). Like Christ, Elias is associated with miraculous bread: "He (=*Elias*) looked, and behold there was at his head a hearth cake[23] and a vessel of water .... And he arose, and ate, and drank, and walked in the strength of that food forty days and forty nights, unto the mount of God, Horeb" (*III Kings* xix; 6,8).

Mr. Holmes (*Graal* 15-16) has already identified the Fisher King and his companion in the boat as Jacob (high priest of the Jewish Temple) and his son Zabulon. There are many references to Jacob in the Holy Week liturgy, in addition to the first several verses of the Lamentations of Jeremias (ch. ii), which have been mentioned *supra*. But, of all the verses which might be applied to the lame Fisher King, perhaps the following are the most striking; they are taken from *Psalm* xxxvii, one of the Penitential Psalms recited both before the Holy Thursday Mass and during Good Friday Matins:

> Rebuke me not, O Lord, in thy indignation: nor chastise me in thy wrath. For thy arrows are fastened in me (*"For he was wounded by a javelin, through both haunches"*: *Perceval*, vv. 3512-3513): and thy hand hath been strong upon me. There is no health in my flesh, because of thy wrath: there is no peace for my bones, because of my sins.... My sores are putrified and corrupted, because of my foolishness. I am become miserable, and am bowed down even to the end: I walked sorrowful all the day long. For my loins are filled with illusions; and there is no health in my flesh (*"Friend, be not offended if I do not arise to greet you, for I am not well"*: *Perceval*, vv. 3107-3109) .... I am ready for scourges, and my sorrow is continually before me" (*does the Fisher King's sorrow consist in his being obliged to witness the symbolic Grail procession without being able to benefit from it?*).

In the Second Nocturn, *Psalm* xxxvii is followed by *Psalm* xxxix, in which v. 13 recalls again the blindness of the Jews: "For evils without number have surrounded me: my iniquities have overtaken me, and I was not able to see." Several verses from the Psalms, in the Third Nocturn, are also applicable to the Fisher King:

> And they shall know that God will rule Jacob: and all the ends of the earth (lviii, 14).

> I am counted among them that go down into the pit: I am become as a man without help (lxxxvii, 5).—Cf. *Perceval*, vv. 3509-3511: "*But in a battle he was wounded and maimed, that is certain, so that he could no longer help himself.*"

> And they have said: The Lord shall not see: neither shall the God of Jacob understand (xciii, 7).

> But the king shall rejoice in God (lxii, 12).

These last words recall the conversation between Perceval and the girl holding the body of the headless knight. When Perceval admits that he has not asked concerning the Grail and the bleeding lance, she exclaims: "How ill-fated you were now, since you did not ask all this! For you would have so helped the good king who is maimed, so that he would have regained (use of) his legs and held his lands; and such great good would have come of it" (vv. 3584-3590). In the Maundy Thursday Matins: "For my days are vanished like smoke: and my bones are grown dry like fuel for the fire" (*Psalm* ci, 4). The Ghimel passage in Lesson I of Good Friday Matins: "And he hath kindled in Jacob as it were a flaming fire devouring round about" (*Lamentations of Jeremias* ii, 3). In the Second Nocturn of Maundy Thursday Matins: "They have set fire to thy sanctuary: they have defiled the dwelling place of thy name on the earth" (*Psalm* lxxiii, 7).

These various references to fire—twice in verses applicable to Jacob and once in connection with the sanctuary—are pertinent when it is remembered that there was a fire (*Perceval*, v. 3093) in the hall of the Grail Castle.

Saint Peter, also, warmed his hands at a fire on the first Holy Thursday night. Is there any connection between Jacob (the Fisher King and High Priest of the Jewish Temple) and Peter (Prince of the Church, and fisherman whom Christ foresaw as fisher of men)? With the dissolution of the Grail Castle, will Jacob give way to Peter? If so, this might account for his garb of sable edged with purple (cf. *Graal* 17).

As for the hermit, does he possibly represent John the Baptist, notably in reflection of the latter's rôle as preacher in the desert (cf. *Matthew* iii)? As Merton says (*Wounds* 120): "It would be hard to exaggerate the importance of St. John the Baptist to the early Cistercians. As far back as St. Benedict, and indeed as the Thebaid, St. John Baptist was regarded as the pattern and patron of monks, and we know that St. Benedict dedicated chapels to him and to St. Martin of Tours on Monte Cassino, after overthrowing the altars of pagan deities there. The piety of our own day is, as a whole, not attracted to the austere Precursor: he is not thought to exercise a sufficient appeal to the heart. But that is far from being true: the thing that most recommends St. John the Baptist to the contemplation of the Cistercian monk or nun is that he really is a model of the love of Christ, a love which is summed up, not in flowery prayers or in pretty sentiments, but in the exultant cry: 'He must increase, and I must decrease!' "

On the other hand, it is the headless knight whom Mr. Holmes (*Graal* 21) has identified with St. John the Baptist, "who lost his head in an endeavor to accomplish a similar quest." Yet, what of identifying this knight with St. Paul, also beheaded, near the Ostian Way? Even the Pauline Epistles, from which Chrétien draws frequently, are written in the virile language of a soldier, with continual references to the armor of God and to the necessity for fighting manfully. Clearly, identifications for the *Perceval* remain at the speculative level!

Perhaps the hideous damsel's *fauve mule* (v. 4612) is to be identified with Mortal Sin (cf. *Graal* 33). One of the Penitential Psalms recited before the Holy Thursday Mass warns against becoming "like the horse and the mule, who have no understanding" (xxxi, 9). Similarly, *Tobias* (vi, 17) refers to "the horse and the mule, which have not understanding; over them the devil hath power." Mr. Holmes calls attention (*Graal* 33) to the circumstance that the lady outside the castle (vv. 3591 ff.) and the hermit (vv. 6339 ff.) "both understand that he (=Perceval) could not ask the questions because of his sin, deriving from the death of his mother. Only the hideous damsel sneers because he failed to take a good chance when it came his way."

In other words, like the horse and the mule, the hideous damsel has no understanding. In Christian symbolism, furthermore, the color of her mule represents deceit: this color, *fauve*, has been analyzed in detail for Old French (including *Perceval*) by Marion A. Greene in *Romance Studies*, XII Chapel Hill, 1950; pp. 75-77); also let it be recalled that Dante consigns the deceivers to the eighth *bolgia* of Hell. The epithets heaped on the hideous damsel (vv. 4624-4632) recall the devils in numerous mediaeval gargoyles; also the ancient notions that the devil appeared in the shape of a lion, leopard, bear, goat, bull, or eagle— to typify his intelligence, strength, cruelty, subtlety. In his *Demonologia* (London, 1827; p. 317), J. S. Forsyth notes a poem attributed to St. Benedict where devils of an inferior order, devils blacker than pitch, were charged with carrying lost souls away from earth; also, Tertullian is cited as calling the devil God's ape. Observe that the hideous damsel in the Chrétien poem is blacker than any iron, notably her neck and hands (vv. 4620-4621). *Psalm* lxxii (v. 23) is included in the Second Nocturn of Holy Thursday Matins: "I am become as a beast before thee." And in Lesson II from the First Nocturn of Holy Saturday Matins: "Their face is now made blacker than coals, and they are not known in the streets; their skin hath stuck to their bones, it is withered, and is become like wood" (*Lamentations of Jeremias* iv, 8). It is plausible that the humps of the hideous damsel would merely represent the further deformity of sin.

Because of his Eucharistic writings, especially his description of the Last Supper, it would be natural to find St. John the Evangelist somewhere in an allegory dealing so extensively with the Blessed Sacrament. The possibility has been suggested in this study that he might be represented by the eagle on top of the sleeping damsel's tent. But, if such is not the case, then it is just possible that he is one of the four servitors who clothe Perceval in his scarlet mantle (cf. vv. 3069-3074), and who pull up the drawbridge behind him. In that event, the other three *valets* might well be the other three Evangelists, and their drawbridge conceivably might be Divine Revelation which serves as span between humanity and divinity. However, speculation of any sort at this point is extremely tenuous.

In regard to the venison (vv. 3280-3289) served at the Grail Banquet (cf. *supra, and Hebrews* ix, 9), Mr. Holmes has called attention (*Graal* 17-18) to passages from *Genesis* and from the Jewish oral law concerning Isaac's fondness for this meat. In this connection, a few lines from the *Pange Lingua* (sixth-century Eucharistic hymn) may also be cited:

>That evening when the supper past
>Which with his brethren was his last,
>The paschal victim having eat
>And closed the law with legal meat,
>He with his hands for food bestows
>Himself, to twelve his wisdom chose,[24]

Again with reference to Perceval's "pre-communion" at the Grail Castle, some passages from the Sequence of the Corpus Christi Mass are apposite:

>Both to good and bad 'tis broken,
>But on each a different token
>Or of life, or death attends:
>Life to good, to bad damnation;
>Lo, of one same manducation
>How dissimilar the ends ....
>Bread, that angels eat in heaven,
>Now becomes the pilgrim's leaven,
>Bread in truth to children given,
>That must ne'er to dogs be thrown.

He, in ancient types disguised (*In figuris praesignatur*),
Was the Isaac sacrificed.

Perhaps the analogies between the Liturgy for Holy Week and the symbols in *Perceval* are neither as numerous nor as deliberate as has been suggested here; perhaps parallels have been pushed too far in some respects. But one thing seems certain, namely that Chrétien's images must have been drawn from the common treasury of religious images that were kept in currency by the Liturgy. It surely is not accident that in the texts for Holy Thursday and Good Friday there appear such a quantity of Chrétien's references: the *fel Giu*, the veil, sacramental penance, manna and the Host, the chalice, the *tailleor*, candles and angels, the bleeding lance, the mournful festival, the Fisher King's black garments edged with purple, his helplessness and the healing remedies, the fire in the castle, the destruction of strongholds, Perceval's silence, the reproach of his conscience followed by contrition and sacramental confession, the Orgueilleux de la Lande, and even the mule of the hideous damsel.

The Cistercian spirit pervades the poem from end to end. As Thomas Merton has said, the twelfth-century Cistercian writers "play only a few variations on the same fundamental theme: the love of God, the knowledge of God in contemplation, the life of virtue, humility, and obedience that prepares the soul for contemplation. Yet, although they are writing most of all of the experience of God, these deeply speculative minds could not pass over their subject without analyzing the nature of charity itself and the make-up of the soul in which this experience was received. The Cistercians were the greatest psychologists of their age. . . . However, since it is not enough to have a soul that is capable of love, and love which is capable of filling it, there must be a Mediator to bring the supernatural love of God down to man and raise him up to God. The Cistercian writers, therefore, find the exemplar, the efficient and meritorious cause of all contemplation in Christ, the Word Incarnate, Who was, in Gilson's happy phrase, 'a concrete ecstasy in Himself'. At the very heart of Cistercian spirituality lies a poignant devotion to the sufferings of Christ and to His death on the Cross. St. Bernard and his disciples entered deeply into the mystery of the Passion—more deeply than any one before their time, except perhaps St. Paul. They saw in the Passion the greatest proof of God's love for men. Constant meditation on Calvary, or rather uninterrupted contemplative awareness of the love of God for men, expressed by His Cross, was one of the characteristics of the interior life of St. Bernard. Compassion for the crucified Saviour was as important a means to dispose the soul for mystical prayer as compassion for one's neighbor" (*Siloe* 28).

That Chrétien did not invent his theme seems certain from his own frequent references to a source-book (cf. *Graal* 29) which may well have been one where the liturgical elements were already partially or wholly present. But, whether this book actually ever existed or not, Chrétien had the story in mind, and wrote it down. It seems to me most probable that he himself introduced most of the liturgical materials from a separate Missal or Holy Week book. He has specifically mentioned Perceval's participation in the Adoration of the Cross and his sacramental confession on Good Friday followed by his sacramental communion on Easter Sunday, thereby emphasizing the liturgical season. And, since it is evident that Chrétien has used the language of the Church, it seems psychologically unsound to suppose that he would apply so much liturgical imagery to any pagan theme. To me it seems inevitable that his theme was identical with that of Holy Church during this particular liturgical season: the conversion of the Jews and of schismatics and heretics; and the idea of the Old Law giving way to the New. This idea is supported by the fact that, not too far removed from Chrétien in time or in space, there was a "Solomon chapel" together with relics of manna and of the lance which figure so prominently in the Grail procession.

The stress on Charity in the prologue, the mother's admonitions, Gornemant's advice, the lament of Blancheflor, the hermit's exhortation at the close of the Perceval story proper: all emphasize the poet's seriousness of purpose in relating an eminently and profoundly Christian tale—a tale which opens and closes with an account of the Passion and the part played in it by the Jews[25]. Chrétien's numerous religious passages would have no point at all if he were merely writing a Celtic story for entertainment[26]. The fondness for Celtic lore which pervaded his earlier works has been made subservient to something more serious. His use of symbolism shows a thorough mastery of the liturgy. Interpreted as a religious allegory, the *Conte del Graal* is a tale of absolute unity and of genuine beauty. Interpreted in any other light, the poem is a disconnected and rather meaningless work in which "there are plenty of inconsistencies (which) point to a multiplicity of defective joints and transitions"[27].

The reader may ask: "Was the *Perceval* a work of atonement for the earlier *Lancelot* written at the behest of Marie de Champagne, and with which Chrétien seems never to have been completely satisfied? If so, why this sudden reform?" As for the first question, possibly so. As for the second, it is not easy to imagine that Chrétien's "reform" was sudden. Perhaps the explanation rests in a response to Mr. Holmes's thought-provoking query: "Why was Chrétien so unproductive between *Yvain* (ca. 1169) and the *Perceval*, a good ten years[28]?" It is my belief that during those ten years Chrétien was experiencing spiritual growth, perhaps even as a Cistercian; that he was learning "to know himself and to know God." Perhaps, like Perceval, he was making a spiritual ascent which begins with contempt of self, passes through fear of God, and terminates in love of God.[29] Perhaps, by recollection and prayer, he was becoming learned in the liturgy and in the truths of his religion. If this be true, the new direction for his final poetic inspiration must have made his choice of theme all but inevitable, in the lofty song which was to be his last.

Sister M. Amelia (Klenke), O.P.
College of St. Mary of the Springs
Columbus, Ohio

In the writing of this essay, I have become indebted to numerous persons. It is with pleasure that I take this opportunity to thank them publicly. That I began this study is due primarily to Professor Urban T. Holmes, Jr., of the University of North Carolina, whose recent articles stirred my curiosity concerning the Judaeo-Christian interpretation of the *Conte del Graal*. That I brought the study to a conclusion is due also in large measure to the following: Reverend Alex. J. Denomy, C.S.B., of the Pontifical Institute of Mediaeval Studies in Toronto; Reverend M. Louis Merton, O.C.R. (Thomas Merton), of Our Lady of Gethsemani Abbey, Kentucky; Professor Edward B. Ham of the University of Michigan; Professor Alexander H. Schutz of the Ohio State University; Professors Henri Peyre, Albert Feuillerat, and Raymond T. Hill, all of Yale University. Although some differed sharply from my conclusions, each has rendered invaluable assistance by reading critically the original version; and then, by extending friendly encouragement or by offering sincere constructive criticism, each has helped to eliminate at least some of the flaws. For errors which persist, I assume full responsibility. To Mr. Ham I owe a special debt of gratitude for having edited and proof-read the final text during my prolonged absence from the States.

Notes

[1] A number of publications are cited fairly frequently in this monograph and, for conciseness of reference, certain bibliographical abbreviations are listed here:
 Perceval.—Der Percevalroman (Li Contes del Graal) von Christian von Troyes, unter benutzung des von Gottfried Baist nachgelassenen handschriftlichen materials, herausgegeben von Alfons HILKA (Halle, Max Niemeyer Verlag, 1932).
 Graal.—Urban T. Holmes, Jr., "A New Interpretation of Chrétien's Conte del Graal," *University of North Carolina Studies in the Romance Languages and Literatures,* VIII (Chapel Hill, 1948). Pp. 36. Note that this publication is a somewhat revised version of Professor Holmes's article of the same title, in *Studies in Philology,* XLIV (1947), 453-476.
 Ardres.—Urban T. Holmes, Jr., "The Arthurian Tradition in Lambert d'Ardres," *Speculum,* XXV (1950), 100-103.
 Siloe.—Reverend M. Louis Merton, O.C.R. (Thomas Merton), *The Waters of Siloe* (New York, 1949).
 Wounds.—Thomas Merton, *What are these Wounds?* (Milwaukee, 1948).
 Liturgia.—Liturgia, Encyclopédie populaire des connaissances liturgiques, publiée sous la direction de l'abbé R. Aigrain (Paris, 1931).

[2] Verses 6292-6295 of *Perceval* read as follows:
 Li fel gïu par lor anvie,
 Qu'an devroit tuër come chiens,
 Firent lor mal et nos granz biens
 Quant il an la croiz le leverent.
It should be noted that, three years later, Hilka preferred the reading of six manuscripts which have *faus* instead of *fel* (v. 6292): this change appears in his edition of *Christian von Troyes, der Percevalroman in auswahl,* in the *Sammlung romanischer Übungstexte* (volumes 26-27, bound as one) published at Halle in 1935.

[3] *Perceval* 3052-3053:
 L'an ne trovast jusqu'a Barut
 Si bele ne si bien assise.
Hilka refers (*Perceval,* page 674) to the line *Muez fusse je pris a Barrut* in the *Bible de Guiot de Provins.* The parallel is of no consequence, except that, as I have been reminded by Professor R. T. Hill of Yale, the verse in Guiot's poem in 2606 and not 2006; Hilka's numbering is incorrect.

[4] Cf. William Bonniwell, O.P., *A History of the Dominican Liturgy* (New York, 1944): "In the Middle Ages, the Ages of Faith, when the people had a deeper knowledge and a better understanding of the liturgy of the Church, their devotional spirit logically sought to express itself in the liturgy" (p. 8). See also *Siloe* 296-298: "The Vulgate became so much a part of the monk's mind that he could not help thinking in its language and seeing things in the light of its symbols and images, and gradually the whole universe became impregnated with the poetry and meaning of scripture . . . . In other words, the Cistercian really worked his way through the liturgy of the fundamental seasons . . . . The mighty lessons taught by the Church in every Nocturn and every Mass had a chance to work themselves right into the blood and marrow of the monk's existence . . . ." As a Cistercian, Merton should know . . . .

[5] In *Wounds* 19, Merton says that "the eagle, according to the usual tradition of mediaeval bestiaries, had the most piercing vision of all creatures, and was supposed to be able to stare straight into the sun without blinking. Also, its powerful wings were able to carry it higher into the heavens than any other bird. It was an obvious symbol of mystical contemplation." And in the Matins of the *Little Office of the Blessed Virgin Mary*: "Happy thou, O sacred Virgin Mary, and most worthy of all praise,

for out of thee arose the Sun of Justice, Christ our God . . . . He hath set His tabernacle in the sun . . . ."

[6] It will be recalled, for instance, that this was one of the last recorded actions of the poet Péguy before his death in the First World War.

[7] From the Matins in the *Little Office of the Blessed Virgin Mary*: "Grace is poured forth on thy lips. Therefore hath God blessed thee forever." In the colors of the tent, Chrétien has the colors *red* and *green* symbolize *love* and *hope*.

[8] Cf. *Graal* 13-17, 29-31, 35. Concerning the identity of Chrétien de Troyes, informative surveys of recent scholarship are to be found in two articles by Raphael Levy: *Medievalia et Humanistica*, VI (1950), 76-83; *Lettres Romanes*, V (1951), 46-52. However, neither of these studies invalidates Mr. Holmes's interpretation of the author's intent in the *Perceval* poem.

[9] Cf. *supra*, note 4. And also, *Siloe* 293: "St. Bernard taught his monks to read Scripture and the Fathers . . . . Searching the sacred text with the eyes of Faith rather than with those of scholarship, they filled their minds and memories with the prophecies and types of Christ in the Old Testament. Then, in the silence of deep and humble meditation they sought to penetrate the surface and slake their thirst at the springs of living water, which only God could lay open to them."

[10] Cf. *Graal* 20; also *Leviticus* xxi, 23, and *II Corinthians* iv, 13ff.

[11] "It is entirely probable that the lance form (for the rod) was used in order to enable Chrétien to continue his allegory further when, at the dissolution of the Grail Castle, the Jewish relics should pass into the most sacred relics of the Passion" (*Graal* 19).

[12] Cf. *Perceval* 6495-6496:
Aprés le servise aora
La croiz et ses pechiez plora.
Also, "Hespelende (a contemporary of St. Lutgarde, in the first part of the thirteenth century) was informed by a prophetic revelation that on Good Friday, at the adoration of the Holy Cross, and at the precise moment when the priest would uncover the Cross singing: 'Ecce lignum Crucis', her temptation would leave her and she would be strengthened by God's grace" (*Wounds* 83).

[13] As Chrétien says that there were at least ten candles in each candlestick, it might be possible to suppose that he chose his number to fit in with the Jewish background he was purportedly painting.

[14] Cf. *Siloe, passim*, and especially the chapter on Cistercian life in the twelfth century. "The need to build a monastery in physical solitude was supplemented by the much more fundamental need for interior solitude and exspoliation. Hence, too, the need for silence, for humility, for fasting, for subjection to superiors (*when reflecting on Perceval's attitude to his mother, which is the direct opposite to all this, one is again forced to wonder about her identity*): all this was to help the monk to divest himself of every selfish desire, every shred of human attachment, because he knew that, once he was empty of self-love (*which Perceval certainly was not*), he would be filled with the love of God" (*Siloe* 281). Note Perceval's complete change of heart by the time he makes his confession to the hermit.

[15] After his own communion during the Good Friday Mass, the priest's concluding prayer asks the Lord to "grant that what we have taken with our mouth, we may receive with a pure heart."

[16] Perceval follows this injunction as his last act in the poem (vv. 6512-6513). During Chrétien's time, incidentally, the Cistercians still received Communion under both species; concerning the suppression of the *sub utraque*, cf. Mme Lot-Borodine, *loc. cit.*, p. 192 (note 2).

[17] Cf. *Liturgia*, pp. 704-705, 711.

[18] Recalling *Hebrews* (iv, 12) and Abelard's explanation for the word of God as a sword, Mr. Holmes (*Graal* 21) shows how "Christ (the word of

God) was sent to Perceval as a sword that would fail him in only one case."
Also, cf. *infra*, concerning Blancheflor.

19 Perceval's loathing to put these garments aside, and his doing so little by little, remind one of *Ecclesiasticus* xix, 1: "And he that contemneth small things, shall fall by little and little."

20 Mr. Holmes has made an excellent start in this direction with his discussions (*Graal* 22-26) of Belrepaire, Clamadeus, Anguingueron, Cotoatre, Trebuchet (cf. also *Graal* 34-35).

21 It has been pointed out, *supra*, that the chastity of Perceval and Blancheflor is established from the *argumentum ex silentio* in the former's confession to the hermit. For the opposite view, cf. Helaine Newstead, *Publications of the Modern Language Association*, LXIII (1948), 827-830; and in particular the note on p. 829. Again concerning the name *Belrepaire*, cf. *Siloe* 272-273: "These valley monasteries developed within the Cistercian Order a beautiful spiritual symbolism by their names alone (*Beaulieu, Bonlieu, Bonport, etc.*), eloquent and harmonious names full of poetry and simple mysticism."

22 Note that Mr. Holmes (*Graal* 24-26) identifies Blancheflor with "Wisdom, Christian Wisdom, as descended from, but opposed to, the Jewish Wisdom of Gornemanz." Thomas Merton has remarked (*Wounds* 33) that "St. Lutgarde's life of penance and reparation was explicitly aimed at the Albigensian heresy"; also, the first of her seven-year fasts, limited to bread and weak beer (*Wounds* 40), is reminiscent of Blancheflor's fare at Belrepaire.

23 "This bread, with which Elias was fed in the wilderness, was a figure of the bread of life which we receive in the blessed sacrament; by the strength of which we are to be supported in our journey through the wilderness of this world till we come to the true mountain of God, and his vision in a happy eternity" (*Douay Version*, Benziger 1914 edition, p. 378, note to *III Kings* xix, 8).

24 Note the parallel between this passage and the principal ideas cited *supra* from the Passion sermon by Pope Leo IX.

25 Cf. *Perceval*, vv. 6364-6367, 6403-6408: "It is full five years that I have not known where I was going; I did not love God, nor believe in God; and in that time I have done naught but evil."—"And you (=*Perceval*) would not have lived so long if she (=*Perceval's mother*) had not commended you to God: this you must know. But her prayer had such virtue that, for her sake, God has cared for you and saved you from death and prison." Compare these verses with the following from St. Bernard (quoted in *Siloe* 293): "Great must be my love for Him through Whom I have existence, life and wisdom. If I am ungrateful to Him, then I am unworthy of Him. Worthy indeed of death is the man who will not live for Thee, Lord Jesus, and he is, in fact, already dead. And the man who has no sense of Who Thou art, is senseless. And the one who desires to live for anything else but Thee is living for nothing and is, himself, nothing. For after all, what is man, if he has no knowledge of Thee?" Perceval at the hermitage and at the moment of his final attainment of faith may be recalled in the following (*Siloe* 291-292): "Meditation and the ways of the interior life were laid open to .... all by a method that transcended every method and obviated all difficulties and all intricacies from the very start. There was nothing involved about it. You came to the (Cistercian) monastery to learn, or rather to relearn, the love whose seeds were implanted in your very nature. And the best way to do this was to open the eyes of faith and gaze upon the perfect embodiment of God's love for men: Christ on the Cross .... St. Bernard transformed and, in some sense, transfigured Christian spirituality by filling it with that lyrical love of Christ and His Virgin Mother which pervades the whole Middle Ages .... Above all, it is only through the merits of Christ's death on the Cross that we can obtain the grace to rise above our own selfishness to the pure and selfless love of God for His own sake, which is the very essence of mysticism for the Cistercians."

²⁶ Chrétien's seriousness of purpose should be compared with the Cistercian idealism in the *Queste del saint Graal*. An observation by Etienne Gilson concerning the latter seems equally applicable to the *Perceval*: "Que *La Queste* soit en outre une oeuvre abstraite et systématique, nous le reconnaissons si complètement, qu'à peine oserions-nous promettre d'y découvrir dix lignes de suite écrites pour le simple plaisir de conter" (*Les Idées et les lettres* [Paris, 1932], pp. 60-61).
²⁷ Helen Adolf, *Modern Language Quarterly*, VIII (1947), 7.
²⁸ *History of Old French Literature*, p. 167.
²⁹ Cf. Gilson, *Les Idées et les lettres*, pp. 49-51.—"The beginning of the ascent is self-knowledge. It is in this atmosphere of humility that the way to contemplation begins . . . . For St. Bernard, the two principal steps in this active preparation were humility and charity" (*Siloe* 22, 24).

The Department of Romance Studies Digital Arts and Collaboration Lab at the University of North Carolina at Chapel Hill is proud to support the digitization of the North Carolina Studies in the Romance Languages and Literatures series.

www.ingramcontent.com/pod-product-compliance
Lightning Source LLC
Chambersburg PA
CBHW020423230426
43663CB00007BA/1288